D0858047

TAYLOR SWIFT

TAYLOR SWIFT

SUPERSTAR SINGER AND SONGWRITER

HEATHER E. SCHWARTZ

LERNER PUBLICATIONS ◆ MINNEAPOLIS

Copyright © 2019 by Lerner Publishing Group, Inc.

All rights reserved. International copyright secured. No part of this book may be reproduced, stored in a retrieval system, or transmitted in any form or by any means—electronic, mechanical, photocopying, recording, or otherwise—without the prior written permission of Lerner Publishing Group, Inc., except for the inclusion of brief quotations in an acknowledged review.

Lerner Publications Company
A division of Lerner Publishing Group, Inc.
241 First Avenue North
Minneapolis, MN USA 55401

For reading levels and more information, look up this title at www.lernerbooks.com.

Image credits: Chris McGrath/TAS/Getty Images, p. 2; Nicky Loh/TAS/Getty Images, pp. 6, 31; Rick Diamond/Getty Images, pp. 8, 9, 16, 18, 20; J. Shearer/WireImage/Getty Images, p. 10; Jesse D. Garrabrant/NBAE/Getty Images, p. 11; Jeff Kravitz/FilmMagic/Getty Images, pp. 15, 25, 29; Chris Walter/WireImage/Getty Images, p. 19; DWD-Media/Alamy Stock Photo, p. 22; Jason Kempin/Getty Images, p. 23; Dan MacMedan/WireImage/Getty Images, p. 26; Music4mix/Shutterstock.com, p. 28; Christopher Polk/AMA2013/Getty Images, p. 33; Gareth Cattermole/TAS/Getty Images, p. 35; Kevin Mazur/BMA2015/WireImage/Getty Images, p. 36; Sammy Smith/WireImage/Getty Images, p. 37; Patti McConville/Alamy Stock Photo, p. 38.

Cover: Kevin Mazur/Getty Images.

Main body text set in Rotis Serif Std 55 Regular 13.5/17. Typeface provided by Adobe Systems.

Library of Congress Cataloging-in-Publication Data

Names: Schwartz, Heather E. author.
Title: Taylor Swift : superstar singer and songwriter / Heather E. Schwartz.
Description: Minneapolis : Lerner Publications, [2019] | Series: Gateway biographies | Includes bibliographical references and index.
Identifiers: LCCN 2018003071 (print) | LCCN 2018002327 (cbook) | ISBN 9781541528864 (eb pdf) | ISBN 9781541528857 (lb : alk. paper)
Subjects: LCSH: Swift, Taylor, 1989 –Juvenile literature | Singers—United States—Biography—Juvenile literature. | Country musicians—United States—Biography—Juvenile literature.
Classification: LCC ML3930.S989 (print) | LCC ML3930.S989 S394 2019 (ebook) | DDC 782.421642092 [B]—dc23

LC record available at https://lccn.loc.gov/2018003071

Manufactured in the United States of America
1-44744-35557-8/29/2018

CONTENTS

Taylor Swift performs at the Singapore Indoor Stadium on June 12, 2014, in Singapore.

All eyes were on the main stage at the 2009 Country Music Awards in Nashville, Tennessee. Faith Hill and Tim McGraw—two of the country music industry's biggest stars—walked to center stage to announce the biggest award of the night: Entertainer of the Year. From her seat in the audience, Taylor Swift watched clips of each nominee performing. For nearly a decade, the award had gone to a male vocalist. For four of the previous five years, it had gone to Kenny Chesney.

Then the moment finally came. "It is our privilege to present tonight's highest honor, the award for Entertainer of the Year," Faith Hill announced. "And the CMA award for Entertainer of the Year goes to . . . Taylor Swift."

She'd won! Her hands covered her face as she stood. Her strapless gown sparkled. Chesney leaned in for a congratulatory hug. Swift later said that as she made her way to the stage, she felt as if she were in a dream. She thought of her second-grade teacher, her crew, her fans— everyone who'd helped her along the way.

Swift *(right)* accepts the award for Entertainer of the Year from Faith Hill and Tim McGraw onstage during the 43rd Annual CMA Awards on November 11, 2009, in Nashville, Tennessee.

"I will never forget this moment, because in this moment, everything that I have ever wanted has just happened to me," she said, tearfully accepting her award.

At the age of nineteen, Swift was only a few short years into her musical career. Yet already, she'd climbed to the top of the charts and had achieved her lifelong dream. Where could she possibly go from here?

"I love a challenge," she told a reporter. "And right now, the challenge is to find that next challenge."

Tapping Her Talent

Taylor Alison Swift was born on December 13, 1989, in West Reading, Pennsylvania. Taylor lived on a Christmas tree farm as a child. She and her younger brother, Austin, grew up riding tractors and playing together.

Taylor's parents, Scott and Andrea Swift, both worked in finance. As a girl, Taylor told people she was going to be a stockbroker or a financial adviser when she got older. After all, her parents had chosen her name because they

Swift (*center*) poses with her parents, Scott and Andrea, at the 48th Annual Academy of Country Music Awards in 2013.

felt it would give her an edge in the corporate world. "My mom thought it was cool that if you got a business card that said, 'Taylor,' you wouldn't know if it was a guy or a girl. She wanted me to be a business person in a business world," Taylor said.

Early on, Taylor showed she wasn't really interested in business, though. She preferred riding horses competitively and listening to country music. Her favorite singers included LeAnn Rimes, Faith Hill, Shania Twain, and the Dixie Chicks. She was drawn not only to their music but to the stories they told in their songs.

LeAnn Rimes performs at the 16th Annual Bridge School Benefit Concert in 2002.

Taylor sings the national anthem before a Philadelphia 76ers basketball game in 2002. She was just twelve years old.

Around the age of nine, Taylor got involved in children's theater but found she liked singing karaoke at the cast parties even better than performing in plays. It's possible she inherited her love of singing from her grandmother, who was a professional opera singer. Taylor was ten when she started singing at fairs and festivals and entering weekend karaoke contests at Pat Garrett's Roadhouse in Bethel, Pennsylvania. She kept going back until she won a year and a half later. Her prize was the opportunity to open for singer Charlie Daniels when he played at an amphitheater near Strausstown, Pennsylvania.

Taylor's passion for singing grew. When she was twelve, she sang the national anthem at a Philadelphia 76ers basketball game. "[Pop star] Jay-Z was sitting courtside and gave me a high-five after I sang," she recalls. "I bragged about that for, like, a year straight."

But while Taylor's early music career was taking off, life at Wyomissing Area Junior High School was far from perfect. She didn't always feel as if she fit in with her classmates. And while her singing made her stand out, it didn't make her more popular. In fact, she lost friends who didn't understand her passion and couldn't connect with her conscientious personality. It was a difficult time for Taylor.

"Anything that makes you different in middle school makes you weird," she later said. "My friends turned into the girls who would stand in the corner and make fun of me."

By then Taylor had an outlet for her pain. She was learning to play guitar and write her own songs. While

Exploring the Business

Taylor started asking her parents to move to Nashville when she was only ten years old. She knew it was the place to be for country singers. When she was eleven, her mother took her to Nashville for a visit. Taylor stopped at several record labels and dropped off demo CDs that featured her singing.

She didn't get a deal out of her trip, but she did learn more about how the business worked. The experience led her to believe that writing her own music was the key to kick-starting her career.

she wasn't immediately great at guitar, she was determined to get better. She played every day after school, putting so much effort into her music that her fingers cracked and bled. In time, she was able to channel her unhappiness into her lyrics. If something bad happened at school, she knew she could use it. She could turn it into a song.

"My life changed so completely when I discovered writing my own songs and playing guitar," she said. "There's nothing I love more than putting words together and making them make sense and working with the cadence or the rhymes at the end of them."

Heading to Hendersonville

Taylor was more than passionate about music. She was driven to succeed and wanted more than anything to sign a deal with a record label. Her trip to Nashville at the age of eleven was far from her only visit there. She went back with new demo CDs that included original songs that showcased both her singing and songwriting abilities. She also auditioned for record labels and heard their rejections firsthand. Executives didn't seem to understand her material. They wanted songs for adults, but she was writing for teenagers.

"A lot of people ask me, how did you have the courage to walk up to record labels when you were twelve or thirteen and jump right into the music industry?" Taylor later said. "It's because I knew I could never feel the kind of rejection that I felt in middle school. Because in the music industry, if they're gonna say no to you, at least they're gonna be polite about it."

Eventually, Taylor found her label and signed a deal with RCA Records at the age of thirteen. But it wasn't quite her dream come true. The company had her sign a development deal, which meant they would help her grow as an artist, but she wouldn't necessarily make an album. Still, she was excited to get her foot in the door. Her whole family relocated so she could work on her career. They bought a house on a lake in Hendersonville, Tennessee. Taylor started going to Hendersonville High School, where she felt accepted by her classmates.

A year later, however, she still hadn't cut an album. The company was starting to pressure her to record other artists' songs. But she wasn't interested. She was determined to write her own material. Finally, she walked away from the deal. It was a risky move but the right one. Sony/ATV Music Publishing quickly signed her to a publishing contract. That meant that she had a job writing her own songs. At fourteen, Taylor was the youngest person the music publishing company had ever signed.

As a songwriter with Sony/ATV Music Publishing, Taylor worked with a partner, an experienced songwriter named Liz Rose. Rose helped Taylor shape catchy ideas and tunes (known in the industry as hooks) into full-fledged songs. She performed the songs around Nashville. Scott Borchetta, a major player in the music industry,

Swift poses with Scott Borchetta (*right*) before the 2006 CMT Music Awards.

noticed her. He was starting his own record label, Big Machine Records, and wanted Taylor Swift on board.

Taylor signed with Big Machine, and the label released her first single, "Tim McGraw," in 2006. The song was filled with ideas to remind a boyfriend of a girlfriend he'd left behind. "The idea for this song came to me in math class. I just started singing to myself, '*When you think Tim McGraw . . .*' The concept for this song hit me because I was dating a guy who moved away, and it was going to be over for us," she said.

To promote the single, she hit the road for six months visiting radio stations. She was on tour, but it wasn't exactly glamorous. "[It was] the most grueling radio tour. Living in hotel rooms, sleeping in the backs of rental cars as my mom drove to three different cities in one day," she said.

Next, Taylor toured as the opening act for country band Rascal Flatts. In October 2006, she released her debut (first) album, *Taylor Swift*, at the age of sixteen. She had a hand in writing all eleven songs on the album, and it went on to sell more than five million copies. Things were working out just the way she'd always dreamed.

From left: Joe Don Rooney, Swift, Gary LeVox, and Jay DeMarcus pose together during the 44th annual Academy of Country Music Awards on April 5, 2009. The men are in the band Rascal Flatts.

Rascal Flatts

Taylor got one of her first big breaks opening for Rascal Flatts. The band included cousins Gary LeVox and Jay DeMarcus along with guitarist Joe Don Rooney. The band got together in the late 1990s and soon landed a record deal. But before they could make it official, they needed a name. A friend suggested they take the name of his old band—Rascal Flatts—from the 1960s.

Since then the band has released eleven studio albums and a string of chart-topping hits. Taylor toured with them on their 2006 Me and My Gang Tour.

A Rising Star

As a professional musician, Swift no longer had time to attend a traditional high school. After tenth grade, she switched to homeschooling for her junior and senior years. The move set her apart from her friends at home. But she knew where she needed—and wanted—to be.

In January 2007, Swift was thrilled to go on tour as the opening act for country singer George Strait. She had plenty of songs ready to go for a second album and even a third. But she found she could also write while on tour. During her downtime, she was often alone. "I do love writing on the road—I usually write at the concert venue.

I'll find a quiet place in some room at the venue, like the locker room," she said.

Opening for major country acts such as Rascal Flatts and George Strait gave Swift a chance to perform in front of huge audiences before she was a major star herself. She began collecting new fans at a fast rate. She sometimes found it hard to believe people were so interested in her and her music.

Swift greets a fan at a 2008 music festival in Twin Lakes, Wisconsin.

"I'm still in the 'Oh-my-gosh-this-is-really-happening' phase," she said. "After all these concerts that I do, people line up and want me to sign things. I still haven't been able to grasp the fact that if I sign a piece of paper, it might mean something to somebody."

In April she joined the tour of country singer Brad Paisley as one of the opening acts. During the tour, she found a friend in Kellie Pickler, another young singer and an opening act. When Pickler got a kitten, the young women bonded as they shared caretaking duties. For Swift, Pickler was like a more experienced older sister. Pickler helped her navigate the relationship drama she wrote about in her songs.

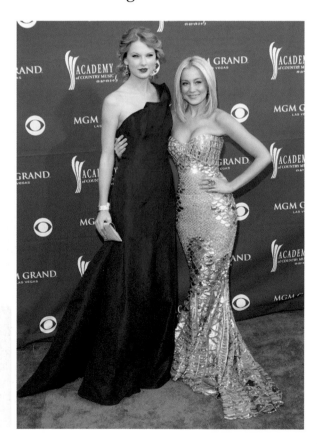

Swift and Kellie Pickler at the 2009 Academy of Country Music Awards at the MGM Grand in Las Vegas on April 5, 2009

"My favorite thing about Kellie is that she's the one person on the planet who has the nerve to delete a guy's number out of my phone if she doesn't think he's right for me," Swift said. "She will grab my phone and delete his number, because she does not want me to talk to someone who she thinks is bad news."

As Swift gained experience, she was becoming a powerful pro. In May 2007, Swift performed her single "Tim McGraw" at the Country Music Awards—with Tim McGraw and his wife, Faith Hill, in the audience. Swift walked right up to them as she played and afterward introduced herself, reaching out confidently to shake McGraw's hand.

Swift performs at the 41st Annual CMA Awards in Nashville, Tennessee, on November 7, 2007.

Something else important happened at the Country Music Awards that night. And it was life changing for Swift. She took home the Horizon Award, an honor given to the new artist who'd shown the most growth over the past year. It was a clear sign she was a developing country music star. Overcome with emotion, she thanked her fans and everyone who'd helped her along the way. Ending her speech, she called the moment the highlight of her senior year.

On a Roll

At the end of 2007, Swift released a six-song Christmas album. On *The Taylor Swift Holiday Collection*, she sang holiday favorites with her own country style.

She was also working toward graduating from high school. Swift managed to complete eleventh and twelfth grades in just one year to graduate early. She was a good student and cared about education, so some wondered whether she'd go on to college.

"Going to college would mean saying goodbye to my music career, and I just can't do that," she said. "There just wouldn't be enough time in the day to be on tour, do interviews, meet-and-greets, TV appearances, and everything else that I need to do and go to college. Maybe later on in life, I'll end up taking a few classes or doing it online. But right now, it just isn't where I need to be."

Swift's 2008 album, *Fearless*

In November 2008, Swift released her second album, *Fearless*. It included twelve tracks, seven of which were her own original songs, written without help from cowriters. Fans loved it. It was the top-selling album of 2009. Soon she was planning a tour to promote the album. This time, Swift would be the headliner, with Pickler as the opening act.

"Headlining my own tour is a dream come true," Swift said. "This way, I can play more music every night than I ever have before. Having written my own songs, they are all stories in my head, and my goal for this tour is to bring those stories to life."

The Fearless Tour launched in April 2009. For the next six months, Swift performed in fifty-two cities in thirty-eight states and provinces throughout the United States and Canada. Swift was beyond sleeping in hotel rooms

Swift performs during the Fearless Tour at Madison Square Garden in New York City on August 27, 2009.

and the backs of rental cars. She had money to invest in her career, and she used it. She bought a penthouse in Nashville for close to $2 million. And she bought a fancy tour bus that would keep her comfortable on the road.

"If I'm spending money, it's gonna be putting it back into my career," she explained. "I don't like to be extravagant any other place. My tour bus is really important because I live there. I'm there more than when I'm home. So, I put a fireplace on my tour bus and a flip-down treadmill and a really comfortable bed. I feel like I'm home whenever I'm on my tour bus. I do not regret that splurge."

Personal Touch

Many musicians keep a professional distance from fans—but not Swift. She's made headlines for both crashing fans' personal space and letting them into hers.

After a meet-and-greet event, Swift surprised one fan by showing up at her bridal shower. She's been known to send fans checks to help with college tuition and even reached into her purse once to pay for a fan's dinner at a Chipotle restaurant. When making her music video for "Shake It Off," she invited fans to be in it too. She even hosted fans at her own home to preview the video for *1989* and enjoy some home-baked cookies.

Country-Pop Crossover

By September 2009, Swift had a well-earned reputation as not only a talented songwriter and singer but as a role model to her fans. In interviews, she talked about how she never drank alcohol and wouldn't lie to her parents. She wasn't interested in partying or doing anything that would cause people to gossip.

"When you lose someone's trust, it's lost," she said, "and there are a lot of people out there who are counting on me right now."

Swift could control her own actions, but she couldn't control what others around her did and said. And on a night that should have been triumphant for her, she got the surprise of her life.

The moment came at the 2009 MTV Video Music Awards. Swift was being honored with the Best Female Video award for her song "You Belong with Me." As she accepted her award and began to speak, rapper Kanye West

Kanye West crashes the stage as Swift accepts her award for the Best Female Video during the MTV Video Music Awards in 2009.

rushed onto the stage and grabbed the microphone from her. West was upset that singer Beyoncé hadn't won the award.

"Yo Taylor, I'm really happy for you, I'll let you finish, but Beyoncé has one of the best videos of all time," he shouted, taking up all the time that had been reserved for her acceptance speech.

Swift sobbed backstage in the five minutes she had before performing her song live. When Beyoncé accepted her own award for Video of the Year, she called Swift onstage to finish her speech. Swift said that she'd always dreamed of winning an award there. But she never thought it would happen, because she was a country music singer, and Video Music Awards typically go to pop stars.

Her award was proof that her music appealed to other music fans in addition to those who enjoyed country. She was a true crossover artist, appealing to both country and pop music fans.

Swift poses with her awards at the 52nd Annual Grammy Awards on January 31, 2010.

At the 2010 Grammy Awards, her place as a fan favorite was solidified. Swift took home four awards, including Best Country Album and Album of the Year for *Fearless*. She won Best Country Song with her writing partner Liz Rose for "White Horse." She also won Best Female Country Vocal Performance for the song.

"Country music is my home. Country music is my love," she said, wearing a shimmering, floor-length blue gown. "But to have it organically cross over this year? It's just been fantastic. I think the healthiest thing you can do when making music is remove stereotypes from it."

Personal Space

As Swift grew more famous, fans clamored to know more about her personal life—especially her boyfriends. Swift didn't disappoint. After dating pop star Joe Jonas from July 2008 to October 2008, she wrote several songs, including "Last Kiss" and "Forever & Always," that were rumored to be about the relationship.

"I like to write personal songs," she said. "I like to write songs that are very obviously about people. It's kind of hard to change your stripes. I like to write songs about love, and I like to write songs about relationships, and I like to write songs about boys."

Living the Good Life

Swift released her third album, *Speak Now*, in October 2010. It was the fastest-selling digital album of all time, according to *Guinness World Records*. With earnings from her songs and tours as well as product endorsements, her annual income was reported to be $45 million.

With that kind of cash, she was able to buy a $2.5 million home for her parents in Nashville. Among their neighbors were singer Keith Urban and actor Nicole

Swift (*top in red*) films a music video on October 29, 2010, in Hollywood, California.

Kidman. Swift also purchased a $3.5 million home for herself in Beverly Hills, California. It had four bedrooms plus a guesthouse and tennis court.

Swift's busy schedule didn't leave her a lot of time to spend in her new home. She hit the road on tour in February 2011 and topped out the year by winning Artist of the Year at the American Music Awards in November.

In 2012 she continued her tour and worked on her fourth album. Still inspired by relationships and love, she packed her songs full of references to recent heartbreaks and raw emotions. Her openness came with risks, but she was willing to take them. While singing "Sparks Fly," for example, she walked through her audience at her concerts.

Swift accepts her Artist of the Year award at the 2011 American Music Awards in Los Angeles, California.

The Truth about Taylor

The media was sometimes overly eager to poke fun at Swift for her failed relationships. In 2013 a newspaper ran a story that labeled Swift as a laughingstock. The story included a photo of Swift crying, presumably over a relationship.

But the photo had been taken at a fund-raising event for sick children. Swift broke down after singing the song "Ronan," which she wrote in memory of a three-year-old boy who died of cancer.

"You know, you get scratched a little bit, but that's nothing to be scared of," she said. "It's really cool to make eye contact with someone while you're singing. To be able to travel through the entire crowd and sort of surprise people who didn't think they were going to get up close to a performance. It's kind of exhilarating actually, walking through a crazy, insane mob of people."

She was also an easy target in the media for jokes about her dramatic reactions and willingness to show emotion. But she was willing to put up with that to get her music out there and make her voice heard. And fans adored her songs. When *Red* was released in October, fans loved Swift's efforts. Sales of the album in the United States soared past a million copies in just one week.

In 2013 Swift bought another property, a $17.75 million mansion in Watch Hill, Rhode Island. With concerts mainly on weekends, she finally had some downtime to spend hosting friends, listening to music, and reading. In March she launched her Red Tour, taking her collection of intense, emotional songs on the road to fans around the world. Some critics called the album her transition into adulthood. Crowds joined her on the journey, singing along to such songs as "I Knew You Were Trouble" and "22."

Swift performs at Singapore Indoor Stadium on June 9, 2014, in Singapore.

A Voice for Change

At the end of 2013, Swift was named Artist of the Year at the American Music Awards, setting a record with her third win in the category. Her reaction was humble and grateful.

"Winning the Artist of the Year for the third time is kind of a little bit mind-numbingly unbelievable," she said. "It's amazing, and the fact that it's fan-voted makes it that much better. I don't expect things to do well by default, so for this to happen is wonderful."

As a powerful player in the music industry, Swift had a voice, and she wasn't afraid to use it. Just a few months before releasing her fifth album, *1989*, she decided to stand out in a new way. She pulled her songs from Spotify, a music streaming service. She stated in a 2014 essay for the *Wall Street Journal* that she didn't believe streaming services paid artists fairly. She continued to fight for artists' rights in 2015, when she wrote an open letter to Apple, criticizing the company for offering customers a trial period during which artists would not be paid for their music.

"This is not about me," she posted on the social media site Tumblr. "Thankfully, I am on my fifth album and can support myself, my band, crew, and entire management team by playing live shows. This is about the new artist or band that has just released their first single and will not be paid for its success. This is about the young songwriter who just got his or her first cut and thought that the royalties [money paid to an artist each time his

Swift accepts the Artist of the Year award during the 2013 American Music Awards on November 24, 2013.

or her song is played] from that would get them out of debt. This is about the producer who works tirelessly to innovate and create."

Her letter had an impact, and Swift put her music back on streaming services only after certain changes were

Silence Breaker

Swift was a strong young woman. But she had a painful secret she kept for years. In 2013 she posed next to a DJ for a photo at an event. Swift says that before she could react, he quickly reached down and grabbed her underneath her skirt. In an instant, it was over. She didn't say anything because she didn't want to take up time and disappoint her fans. She only told her team later, and the DJ was fired.

Years later, though, Swift spoke out in court about what had happened. She stood her ground when the DJ denied grabbing her and tried to sue her for $3 million over the loss of his job. When the DJ's lawyer asked if she felt guilty, she answered, "I'm not going to let you or your client make me feel in any way that this is my fault. Here we are years later, and I'm being blamed for the unfortunate events of his life that are the product of his decisions—not mine."

Not only did Swift win in court, she was also named one of *Time* magazine's Silence Breakers of 2017—a list of people who've spoken out about sexual abuse.

made. Apple Music agreed to pay royalties to artists even during a free trial. And Spotify created an option for artists to keep their music off the free tier during the first two weeks.

Swift also worked to help people in other ways. In 2015 she donated $50,000 to a fan with cancer who had to miss a concert and another $50,000 to one of her backup dancer's nephews, who was also fighting cancer. And she gave $50,000 to the Seattle Symphony and the

Swift meets fans in London, England, after kicking off the European leg of her blockbuster Red Tour with the first of five sold-out shows on February 1, 2014.

same amount to fund arts education in New York City schools. At the end of the year, she topped the charitable organization DoSomething.org's Celebs Gone Good list. She has topped the list in many other years as well.

Swift's career was having an impact on the world. And she made another list in 2015 too. At the age of twenty-five, she was named one of *Forbes*'s 100 Most Powerful Women in the World.

Forward Motion

Early 2016 was a time of change for Swift. She had a new single, "Out of the Woods"; a new boyfriend, record producer Calvin Harris; and a new look—a bob haircut.

She debuted her new haircut at the Grammy Awards, where she won Album of the Year for *1989*, among other honors. And she was in another public feud with Kanye West, who was claiming

Swift and Calvin Harris attend the 2015 Billboard Music Awards in Las Vegas, Nevada, on May 17, 2015.

Swift shows off a new haircut at the 58th Grammy Awards on February 15, 2016.

his bad behavior years before was the real reason for her success. He claimed that his actions at the awards show at that time drew attention to Swift and increased her fame. As she accepted her award, Swift was quick to correct him.

"I want to say to all of the young women out there, there are going to be people along the way who will try to undercut your success or take credit for your accomplishments or your fame," she said. "But if you just focus on the work, and you don't let those people sidetrack you, someday, when you get where you're going, you'll look around and you'll know that it was you and the people that love you that put you there. And that will be the greatest feeling in the world."

Swift's rise to fame came with more than a few bumps in the road. When she needed to, she spoke up for herself

Swift on Social Media

By 2017 Swift had 250 million followers on Twitter, Instagram, and Facebook. And that year, she shocked them all. First, she kept performing to a minimum. Instead, she spent time in Nashville, away from the drama of her very public life. Then, in August, she wiped her social media accounts clean. When she returned online a few days later, she was a new Swift with a new album, *Reputation*. It was all about reinventing herself as an artist.

Instead of talking to TV reporters and magazine writers about it, she shared the news directly with fans on social media. *Reputation* quickly hit No. 1 on the Billboard chart, proving that Swift no longer needed to rely on traditional promotion to sell her music.

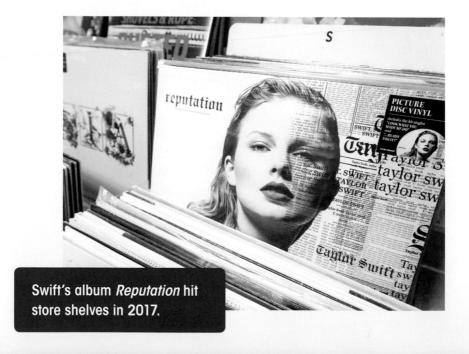

Swift's album *Reputation* hit store shelves in 2017.

and for others. But through it all, she remained true to her values. She worked hard to keep her focus and continue sharing her music with the world. And with her talent and passion, Swift seems likely to be winning over music fans for years to come.

IMPORTANT DATES

1989 Taylor Swift is born on December 13 in West Reading, Pennsylvania.

2006 She releases her first single, "Tim McGraw."

2007 She wins the Horizon Award at the Country Music Awards.

2008 She releases her second album, *Fearless.*

2009 She is named Entertainer of the Year at the Country Music Awards.

2010 She takes home four Grammy awards and releases her third album, *Speak Now.*

2013 She is named Artist of the Year for the third time at the American Music Awards.

2014 She challenges streaming services, including Spotify, claiming that the services pay artists unfairly for their work.

2015 She is named one of *Forbes*'s 100 Most Powerful Women in the World.

2017 She releases her sixth album, *Reputation*.

She is named one of *Time* magazine's Silence Breakers of 2017.

2018 She begins her Taylor Swift's Reputation Stadium Tour.

SOURCE NOTES

7   "Taylor Swift Wins Entertainer of the Year (CMA 2009)," YouTube video, 3:11, posted by "smiley92," November 12, 2009, https://www.youtube.com/watch?v=FmmFPQagsNc.

8   "Taylor Swift Sweeps Country Music Awards 2009," YouTube video, 1:58, posted by Artisan News Service, November 12, 2009, https://www.youtube.com/watch?v=vMTTaAR3xtg.

8   "Taylor Swift Backstage at the 2009 CMA Awards," YouTube video, 9:24, posted by WAAY Huntsville, November 12, 2009, https://www.youtube.com/watch?v=-ctGZEEsTpk.

10   Vanessa Grigoriadis, "The Very Pink, Very Perfect Life of Taylor Swift," *Rolling Stone*, March 5, 2009, http://www.rollingstone .com/music/news/the-very-pink-very-perfect-life-of-taylor -swift-20090305.

11   Cmt.com staff, "20 Questions with Taylor Swift," CMT, November 12, 2007, http://www.cmt.com/news/1574118/20-questions-with -taylor-swift.

12   Grigoriadis, "Very Pink."

13   Cmt.com staff, "Taylor Swift Education Center Opens," CMT, October 14, 2013, http://www.cmt.com/news/1715573/taylor -swift-education-center-opens/.

13–14   Chris Willman, "Taylor Swift's Road to Fame," *EW*, February 5, 2008, http://ew.com/article/2008/02/05/taylor-swifts-road-fame/.

15   Gayle Thompson, "11 Years Ago: Taylor Swift's Debut Album Is Released," Boot, October 24, 2017, http://theboot.com/taylor -swift-debut-album-released/.

15   Rory Evans, "Interview with Taylor Swift: She's Living Her Taylor-Made Dream," *Women's Health*, November 3, 2008, https://www.womenshealthmag.com/life/taylor-swift-interview.

17–18   Dale Kawashima, "Special Interview (2007): Taylor Swift Discusses Her Debut Album, Early Hits, and How She Got Started," SongwritersUniverse February 16, 2007, http://www.songwriteruniverse.com/taylorswift123.htm.

19   Edward Morris, "When She Thinks 'Tim McGraw,' Taylor Swift Savors Payoff," CMT, December 1, 2006, http://www.cmt.com/news/1546980/when-she-thinks-tim-mcgraw-taylor-swift-savors-payoff/.

20   Pat Gallagher, "Kellie Pickler Gives Tough Love to 'Sister' Taylor Swift," Boot, accessed June 10, 2018, http://theboot.com/kellie-pickler-gives-tough-love-to-sister-taylor-swift/.

21   Cmt.com staff, "20 Questions."

22   Cmt.com staff, "Taylor Swift Announces First National Tour as Headliner," CMT News, January 30, 2009, http://www.cmt.com/news/1603909/taylor-swift-announces-first-national-tour-as-headliner.

24   "Taylor Swift: My Biggest Splurge Is My Tour Bus," Just Jared, November 11, 2008, http://www.justjared.com/2008/11/11/taylor-swift-glamour-women-of-the-years-awards/.

25   Grigoriadis, "Very Pink."

26   Daniel Kreps, "Kanye West Storms the VMAs Stage during Taylor Swift's Speech," *Rolling Stone*, September 14, 2009, https://www.rollingstone.com/music/news/kanye-west-storms-the-vmas-stage-during-taylor-swifts-speech-20090913.

27   Ann Donahue, "Beyonce, Taylor Swift Score Big at 2010 Grammy Awards," *Billboard*, January 31, 2010, https://www.billboard.com/articles/news/959533/beyonce-taylor-swift-score-big-at-2010-grammy-awards.

27 Jocelyn Vena, "Taylor Swift Says She Owed It to Her Fans to Be Open about Joe Jonas Breakup," *MTV*, November 10, 2008, http://www.mtv.com/news/1599032/taylor-swift-says-she-owed-it-to-her-fans-to-be-open-about-joe-jonas-breakup/.

30 Patrick Doyle, "Backstage with Taylor Swift on Her Huge Summer Stadium Tour," *Rolling Stone*, August 1, 2013, https://www.rollingstone.com/music/news/backstage-with-taylor-swift-on-her-huge-summer-stadium-tour-20130801.

32 "Taylor Swift on Winning 'Artist of the Year' at the 2013 AMA's," YouTube video, 2:55, posted by HitFix, November 25, 2013, https://www.youtube.com/watch?v=bxDqyCOhR2U.

32, 34 Kaitlyn Tiffany, "A History of Taylor Swift's Odd, Conflicting Stances on Streaming Services," Verge, June 9, 2017, https://www.theverge.com/2017/6/9/15767986/taylor-swift-apple-music-spotify-statements-timeline.

37 Alyssa Bailey, "The Year in Taylor Swift," *Elle*, December 13, 2016, http://www.elle.com/culture/celebrities/news/a41384/the-year-in-taylor-swift-2016/.

SELECTED BIBLIOGRAPHY

Bryant, Kenzie. "How Taylor Swift's Fourth of July Party Became the Ultimate Symbol of Good, Clean, Famous Fun." *Vanity Fair*, June 30, 2017. https://www.vanityfair.com/style/2017/06/taylor-swift-fourth -of-july-rhode-island-party-2017.

Cherrington, Rosy. "10 Ridiculously Cool Things Taylor Swift Has Done for Her Fans." *Telegraph* (London), June 22, 2015. http://www .telegraph.co.uk/culture/music/rockandpopmusic/11439611/10 -ridiculously-cool-things-Taylor-Swift-has-done-for-her-fans.html.

CMT.com staff. "20 Questions with Taylor Swift." CMT, November 12, 2007. http://www.cmt.com/news/1574118/20-questions-with-taylor -swift/.

Grigoriadis, Vanessa. "The Very Pink, Very Perfect Life of Taylor Swift." *Rolling Stone,* March 5, 2009. https://www.rollingstone.com/music /news/the-very-pink-very-perfect-life-of-taylor-swift-20090305.

Kreps, Daniel. "Kanye West Storms the VMAs Stage during Taylor Swift's Speech." *Rolling Stone*, September 14, 2009. https://www .rollingstone.com/music/news/kanye-west-storms-the-vmas-stage -during-taylor-swifts-speech-20090913.

Lewis, Randy. "'I Feel like I'm in a Dream'—Taylor Swift, CMA 2009 Entertainer of the Year." *Los Angeles Times*, November 11, 2009. http://latimesblogs.latimes.com/music_blog/2009/11/i-feel-like-im-in -a-dreamtaylor-swift-cma-entertainer-of-the-year.html.

Martino, Andy. "Exclusive: The Real Story behind Taylor Swift's Guitar 'Legend': Meet the Computer Repairman Who Taught the Pop Superstar How to Play." *New York Daily News*, January 10, 2015. http://www.nydailynews.com/entertainment/music/computer-tech -taught-taylor-swift-guitar-exclusive-article-1.2072638.

"Rare Phots of Taylor Swift before Fame." *New York Daily News*, January 10, 2015. http://www.nydailynews.com/entertainment /photographer-reveals-rare-photos-taylor-swift-international-star

-gallery-1.2072369?pmSlide=1.2072340.

Widdicombe, Lizzie. "You Belong with Me." *New Yorker*, October 10, 2011. https://www.newyorker.com/magazine/2011/10/10/you-belong -with-me.

Willett, Megan. "Take a Tour of Taylor Swift's Many Homes across America." *Business Insider*, January 25, 2017. http://www .businessinsider.com/photos-tour-taylor-swift-house-2017-1.

FURTHER READING

BOOKS

Niver, Heather Moore. *Taylor Swift: Singer and Songwriter*. New York: Enslow, 2018. Learn more about how early ambition took Swift to the top.

Omoth, Tyler. *Taylor Swift: Music Icon*. Mankato, MN: Child's World, 2017. Read about Swift's rise to stardom.

Schwartz, Heather E. *Beyoncé: The Queen of Pop*. Minneapolis: Lerner Publications, 2019. Read about another powerful icon in music.

WEBSITES

Billboard
https://www.billboard.com/music/taylor-swift
Find out which of your favorite Taylor Swift tunes made music chart history.

Grammy Awards
https://www.grammy.com
Is Swift up for any Grammy Awards? Check here!

Taylor Swift
https://taylorswift.com
Do you want to know more about Swift's music and tours? Get info straight from the source on the singer's official website.

INDEX